JeALOUSy
and the
BLINDNESS *of*
BIBLICAL
BETRAYAL

JEALOUSY
and the
BLINDNESS *of*
BIBLICAL
BETRAYAL

THE NEGATIVE POWER OF JEALOUSY IN LEADERSHIP AND LIFE

BISHOP F. JOSEPHUS (JOEY) JOHNSON, II

XULON PRESS

Xulon Press
2301 Lucien Way #415
Maitland, FL 32751
407.339.4217
www.xulonpress.com

Unless otherwise indicated, Scripture quotations taken from the New American Standard Bible (NASB). Copyright © 1960, 1962, 1963, 1968, 1971, 1972, 1973, 1975, 1977, 1995 by The Lockman Foundation. Used by permission. All rights reserved.

Scripture quotations taken from the Holy Bible, New Living Translation (NLT). Copyright ©1996, 2004, 2007 by Tyndale House Foundation. Used by permission of Tyndale House Publishers, Inc.

Printed in the United States of America.

ISBN-13: 978-1-6305-0287-4

CONTENTS

Table of Contents

PREFACE

In my book, The *Blindness of Biblical Betrayal*, I give a short treatment of René Girard's thesis of "mimetic rivalry." "René Girard was the world's premier thinker about the role of violence in cultural origins, and about the Bible's illumination of these origins and our present human condition."[1] He wrote nearly 30 books that cover many academic domains. In addition, there is a large and growing body of secondary literature on his work and influence that touches on such disciplines as literary criticism, critical theory, anthropology, theology, psychology, mythology, sociology, economics, cultural studies, and philosophy.

Mimetic rivalry is the acquisitive desire for what others desire. This unconscious

---

[1] Girard, Rene, *I See Satan Fall Like Lightning*. (Page 11) Orbis Books. Kindle Edition.

mechanism of imitative desire forms our desires. We also considered how those we imitate may be our models, rivals, or obstacles. We touched on how mimetic rivalry can lead to betrayal and engenders blindness that attends such betrayal. We then applied the teaching to a few examples and pointed out, in the words of Girard, "We are never more blind than when we are doing violence in the name of God."

In this book, we'll explore the impact of mimetic rivalry in the most extensive and paradigmatic biblical story of betrayal, i.e. the story of King Saul and David.

King Saul was the first king of the twelve tribes of Israel. Although Saul was physically impressive, he was a spiritual failure.

David followed Saul as king of Israel and became one of her most celebrated kings. God took a forgotten shepherd boy and made him king.

We'll see the jealousy that drives King Saul and we'll know that "We are never more blind or violent than when jealousy is driving us!"

INTRODUCTION

While my book The Blindness of Biblical Betrayal was going to print (May 2019), I was doing my usual devotional reading. I read through the Bible once a year and have read through the Bible more than 40 times.

I was using a resource entitled *Every Day with Jesus: Daily Bible*. The reading for the day was in 1 Samuel. The reading began to unfold the story of the rivalry between King Saul and David. The more I read, the more the Spirit began to reveal to me that the story of King Saul and David is the quintessential story of biblical betrayal.

I noticed that the story is relayed in more than 20 long chapters. We'll use these biblical chapters as the basis for this book. This intrigued me and I began to wonder, why would God choose to give so much biblical text to this Old Testament story of betrayal.

Well, I could think of a number of reasons: 1) King David is the most celebrated King of Israel; 2) King David is a foil that is used to highlight the failure of the kings of Israel and the failure of Israel to be the people that God had envisioned; 3) there are many lessons that God wants us to learn from his life. But there is another powerful reason that the Spirit revealed to me: the story of King Saul's jealousy and betrayal is paradigmatic. In King Saul, we can see the serpent in the Garden of Eden, Cain's jealousy of Abel, the devil's jealousy of the unique Son of God, the enmity of the Antichrist, etc., etc., etc.

A very small incident, singing women who attributed the killing of tens of thousands to David and only thousands to King Saul precipitated suspicion in King Saul and he kept a jealous eye on David from that day forward, because he believed that David was after his throne.

From that day forward, King Saul chased David all over the countryside with the purpose of killing him. In my book, *The Blindness of Biblical Betrayal*, we covered imitative rivalry and the quote by Girard, "We are never more blind than when we are doing violence in the name of God!"

In this book, we'll apply what we learned in *The Blindness of Biblical Betrayal*, and we'll learn, "We are never more blind and violent than when jealousy is driving us!"

CHAPTER 1

SAUL CHOSEN TO BE KING

1 Samuel 9:1-27

To understand the scope of Saul's betrayal of David, God has chosen to give us a panoramic view of Saul's life. In 1 Samuel 9:1-27, God chooses Saul to be king of Israel.

To begin Saul's story, we learn that he is very handsome and from the head up is taller than any of the people.

Somehow Kish's donkeys, Kish was Saul's father, got lost. Kish sent Saul, along with one of his servants, to look for the donkeys.

Saul and his father's servant searched so long for the donkeys that Saul became concerned that his father would begin to worry about them.

Since they were close to the city where the man of God lived, they decided to go and see if he had any word about the donkeys.

The circumstances brought them into contact with Samuel, the last of the judges and the first of the prophets.

God revealed to Samuel that Saul was His choice to be king over His people. So, Saul ate with Samuel that day.

Remember: God did not want to give the Israelites a king, rather they rejected God's governance and wanted a king like the nations around them.

This is important background to the story of Saul and David.

CHAPTER 2

SAUL'S PROPHETIC EXPERIENCE AND PUBLIC ANOINTING

1 Samuel 10:1-27

The next day after Saul ate with Samuel, before sending them away, Samuel privately anointed Saul as king and gave him several prophecies. Then he instructed Saul to go to Gilgal ahead of him and wait for him. He instructed Saul to wait for him for seven days and then he would come and show him what he should do.

When Saul turned around to leave Samuel, all the signs came about in one day. In addition, Saul encountered a group of prophets; and the

Spirit of God came upon him mightily and he began to prophesy among them.

These two events are attached to Saul becoming king: he was anointed with oil and the Holy Ghost.

While they were in town, Saul's uncle asked him about what had happened as he searched for the donkeys. Saul told his uncle how Samuel had shared that the donkeys had been found, but he did **not** share about the prophecies that Samuel had given him related to him becoming king.

After this, Samuel called the people together, before the LORD, at Mizpah. He charges them with rejecting God by asking for a king and instructs them to present themselves before the LORD. He cast lots to see who would be chosen as king. Casting lots was the Israelites' way of affirming God's instructions. We're not sure whether casting lots was like drawing sticks or casting dice, but it was their way of hearing from God.

Perhaps it's best to read the text for the next occurrences.

> 1 Samuel 10:20-24 (NASB), "[20] Thus Samuel brought all the tribes of Israel near, and the tribe

of Benjamin was taken by lot. [21] Then he brought the tribe of Benjamin near by its families, and the Matrite family was taken. And Saul the son of Kish was taken; but when they looked for him, he could not be found. [22] Therefore they inquired further of the Lord, 'Has the man come here yet?' So the Lord said, 'Behold, he is hiding himself by the baggage.' [23] So they ran and took him from there, and when he stood among the people, he was taller than any of the people from his shoulders upward. [24] Samuel said to all the people, 'Do you see him whom the Lord has chosen? Surely there is no one like him among all the people.' So all the people shouted and said, '*Long* live the king!'"

Samuel told the people the rights and duties of kingship, wrote them in a book, and placed them before the Lord.

Samuel dismissed the people and went to his house at Gibeah. Some of the valiant men, whose hearts had been touched by God, went with him.

Now certain worthless men despised Saul, berated him, and did **not** bring any present to honor him. But Saul kept silent.

The plot thickens, as we move toward the betrayal of David by Saul.

CHAPTER 3

SAUL DEFEATS THE AMMONITES

1 Samuel 11:1-15

Saul's reign begins with great promise. After the Spirit of God came mightily upon him, he delivered Israel from their Ammonite enemies with a small group of soldiers.

In the light of God's deliverance through Saul, the people demanded that those who had despised, berated, and dishonored Saul be put to death.

But Saul intervened and said, "Not a man shall be put to death today, for God has accomplished deliverance in Israel."

So, Samuel and all the people went to Gilgal and made Saul king before the LORD. They offered peace offerings and rejoiced greatly!

With such a wonderful beginning, it's difficult to pick up on the signs of trouble in the future.

This background will add texture to our understanding of the betrayal that is coming.

CHAPTER 4

SAUL'S UNLAWFUL SACRIFICE

For His own purposes, God has chosen to have this long story recorded for us. Remember: the Bible was written **for** us, but it was not written **to** us. It was written to a different people, at a different time, in a difficult culture, with a different logic. But God wants us, His people, to learn how to walk in intimate relationship with Him.

God is giving us the background of the paradigmatic betrayer and betrayal in the Bible.

In this chapter we are given details of Saul's reign and a telling incident.

Saul was 30 years old when he began to reign, and he reigned 42 years over Israel.

The Philistines are the perennial Old Testament enemy of Israel. *Wikipedia* says that the Hebrew term for "Philistine" occurs 286 times in the Masoretic Text of the Hebrew Bible. 152 of those occurrences are in 1 Samuel.

Saul had 3,000 special soldiers stationed with him. 2,000 of them were with Saul in Michmash and in the hill country of Bethel. 1,000 were with his son Jonathan at Gibeah of Benjamin. The rest of the people he sent to their tents.

It so happens that Jonathan smote the garrison of Philistines that was at Geba. The news spread quickly among the Philistines. This caused the Philistines to hate the Israelites more than ever. So, Saul blew the rams' horn to summon the army for battle and the entire Israelite army joined Saul in Gilgal.

Now, the Philistines amassed a mighty army at Michmash. When the Israelite soldiers saw what distress they were in, they tried to hide in caves, thickets, rocks, holes, and cisterns. Some crossed the Jordan River and escaped that way.

Meanwhile, Saul stayed at Gilgal and waited seven days for Samuel, as he had previously been instructed. Unfortunately, Samuel didn't arrive when expected and the troops were slipping away.

Saul was so desperate that he offered the burnt offering himself.

Now, as soon as he finished offering the burnt offering, Samuel arrived!

Saul went out to greet Samuel, but Samuel said, "What have you done!"

Saul explained that when the troops were scattering, he felt compelled to offer the burnt offering.

Samuel rebuked Saul for his foolishness in **not** keeping the command of the LORD. Saul evidently disobeyed on two accounts. First, he didn't wait for Samuel as Samuel had instructed. Second, he violated the separation between kingship and priesthood. Apparently, the Canaanites observed a priest-king model and Saul followed that model purposely or inadvertently.

This disobedience reveals something essential about Saul and his character. We can't quite see what is revealed yet, but it may be pride. At any rate, Saul was more concerned with his own agenda than he was obeying God.

We are learning some things about the man who will betray David.

Samuel informs Saul that if he had kept the command of God then God would have established his kingdom forever. But since he hadn't, his kingdom must end, and God had already appointed a new king after His own heart.

Samuel went up to Gilgal, but Saul and the army went up to meet the Philistines.

When Saul counted his men, only 600 were left and they were ill-equipped to do battle with Philistines, who had already secured the pass at Michmash.

CHAPTER 5

KING SAUL'S FOOLISH VOW AND CONSTANT WARFARE

1 Samuel 14:1-52

One day Jonathan and his armor decided to attack a Philistine outpost, but Jonathan didn't tell his father what he was doing.

No one knew that Jonathan and his armor bearer had left camp.

As they approached the outpost, Jonathan makes a Gideon-like fleece, the text reads in

> 1 Samuel 14:8-10 (NASB), "⁸ Then Jonathan said, 'Behold, we will cross over to the men and reveal ourselves to them. ⁹ If they say to

us, "Wait until we come to you"; then we will stand in our place and not go up to them. [10] But if they say, "Come up to us," then we will go up, for the L ORD has given them into our hands; and this shall be the sign to us.'"

Well, the Philistines said, "Come up to us!" Earlier, Jonathan had said, "Who knows whether God will save by few or by many." He now said to his armor bearer, "Come behind me, because the L ORD will help us defeat them."

Jonathan killed about 20 men and this caused panic to break out among the Philistines.

When Saul and those with him saw that the Philistines troops were dwindling away, Saul ordered a roll call to see who was missing. It was then that they found out that Jonathan and his armor bearer were missing.

The text reads in

1 Samuel 14:20-23 (NLT2), "[20] Then Saul and all his men rushed out to the battle and found the Philistines killing each other. There was terrible confusion everywhere. [21] Even the Hebrews

who had previously gone over to the Philistine army revolted and joined in with Saul, Jonathan, and the rest of the Israelites. [22] Likewise, the men of Israel who were hiding in the hill country of Ephraim joined the chase when they saw the Philistines running away. [23] So the LORD saved Israel that day, and the battle continued to rage even beyond Beth-aven."

Now the troops became exhausted because Saul had commanded that no one eat until he had full revenge on his enemies, but Jonathan did not hear the command, because he was not with the army when it was made.

Consequently, Jonathan dipped his spear in some honey that was on the ground and was refreshed.

One of the soldiers saw him eat the honey and informed him of the command that Saul had given. Jonathan commented on the foolishness of the command.

After fighting all day, the men rushed upon the spoil and began to eat meat with blood in it, which was forbidden in the Law of Moses.

Saul commanded that the troops bring the meat to a rock and drain the blood from the meat.

So, Saul decided to continue to chase the Philistines, but he wanted to inquire of the LORD first. But when he inquired of the LORD there was no answer.

Saul began to ask the leaders what sin had been committed, but no one would tell him what was wrong.

Saul vowed that even it was Jonathan who was responsible he would die.

They cast lots and the lots pointed out Jonathan.

Saul said to Jonathan, "Tell me what you have done."

Jonathan explained what happened with the honey and Saul declared that Jonathan must die!

Providentially, the people interceded for Jonathan! The text reads in

> 1 Samuel 14:45 (NASB), "[45] But the people said to Saul, 'Must Jonathan die, who has brought about this great deliverance in Israel? Far from it! As the LORD lives, not one hair of his head shall fall to the ground, for he has

worked with God this day.' So the people rescued Jonathan and he did not die."

This chapter goes on to summarize Saul's military victories.

Then it lists Saul's family.

Finally, we get a summary statement of Saul's warfare against the Philistines.

1 Samuel 14:52 (NASB), "[52] Now the war against the Philistines was severe all the days of Saul; and when Saul saw any mighty man or any valiant man, he attached him to his staff."

CHAPTER 6

KING SAUL'S DISOBEDIENCE CONCERNING THE AMALEKITES

1 Samuel 15:1-34

Now we come to another telling incident in the life of Saul.

Samuel approached Saul with a word from the LORD. That word is recorded in

> 1 Samuel 15:2-3 (NASB), "² Thus says the LORD of hosts, 'I will punish Amalek *for* what he did to Israel, how he set himself against him on the way while he was coming up from Egypt. ³ Now

go and strike Amalek and utterly destroy all that he has, and do not spare him; but put to death both man and woman, child and infant, ox and sheep, camel and donkey.'"

What Amalek did to Israel is recorded in

Deuteronomy 25:17-19 (NASB), "[17] Remember what Amalek did to you along the way when you came out from Egypt, [18] how he met you along the way and attacked among you all the stragglers at your rear when you were faint and weary; and he did not fear God. [19] Therefore it shall come about when the LORD your God has given you rest from all your surrounding enemies, in the land which the LORD your God gives you as an inheritance to possess, you shall blot out the memory of Amalek from under heaven; you must not forget."

Although there's not enough history given to be certain, the words "Amalek" and "Rephidim" can mean giant. So, Amalek may have been a part of the giants that were born from the sin of the sons of God in Genesis 6:1-4. The giants were not just against God's people, they were against God. This may explain why God states that He is at war with Amalek and they are to be wiped out.

Then Saul summoned the people, numbered them, and set an ambush against the city of Amalek. The unusually large number can be explained by a misunderstanding of the terminology or their custom of inflating numbers for the purpose of intimidation, but that is a topic for a different book.

Saul defeated the Amalekites, captured their king, Agag, and killed the people. This seems unusually cruel and there are different ways to read this text, but again, that is the topic for different book.

Now comes a "but" that is very revealing. The text reads in

> 1 Samuel 15:9 (NASB), "[9] But Saul and the people spared Agag and the best of the sheep, the oxen, the fatlings, the lambs, and all that was good, and were not willing to destroy them utterly; but

everything despised and worthless, that they utterly destroyed."

Then the word of the LORD came to Samuel, saying, "I regret that I have made Saul king, for he has not been loyal to me and he has refused to obey my commands." Saul was deeply disturbed when he heard this, and he cried out to the LORD all night.

If that wasn't bad enough, the next morning Samuel went to find Saul, and someone told him that Saul had gone to Carmel to set up a monument to himself and then Samuel went down to Gilgal.

Are you following this story? **Saul has disobeyed God twice and now it seems that he has set up a monument to himself.** We are learning a great deal about Saul's character. His disobedience seems to be connected to pride and this monument also points to pride.

When Samuel approached Saul, Saul blesses him and proclaims, "I have carried out the command of the LORD." Whereas, Samuel responds, "Then what is this bleating of sheep and lowing of oxen that I hear?" Saul blames the people for sparing the best of the livestock to sacrifice to the LORD.

Samuel says, "Let me tell you what God said to me last night." Saul says, "Tell me."

Samuel speaks for the Lord. The wording is important, so let's cite it.

> 1 Samuel 15:17-19 (NASB), "[17] Samuel said, 'Is it not true, though you were little in your own eyes, you were *made* the head of the tribes of Israel? And the Lord anointed you king over Israel, [18] and the Lord sent you on a mission, and said, "Go and utterly destroy the sinners, the Amalekites, and fight against them until they are exterminated." [19] Why then did you not obey the voice of the Lord, but rushed upon the spoil and did what was evil in the sight of the Lord?'"

Saul again attempts to blame the people, and Samuel gives some very pointed words.

> 1 Samuel 15:22-23 (NASB), "[22] Samuel said, 'Has the Lord as much delight in burnt offerings and sacrifices As in obeying the voice of the Lord? Behold, to obey is better

than sacrifice, *And* to heed than the fat of rams. [23] For rebellion is as the sin of divination, And insubordination is as iniquity and idolatry. Because you have rejected the word of the LORD, He has also rejected you from *being* king.'"

Although Samuel begins with a question, the message is clear.

God wanted loyal obedience, not burnt offerings and sacrifices.

To obey is better than sacrifice and to listen to the voice of the LORD is better than the offering of the fat of rams in sacrifice

Rebelling is as the sin of divination, because the rebellious person divines his own way as opposed to God's will.

Insubordination is as filthiness and idolatry.

Then comes the consequences, "Because you have rejected the word or command of the LORD, He has rejected you from being king."

In the next verse, in the confession of Saul, we learn even more about his sin and his mindset. The text reads

1 Samuel 15:24 (NASB), "[24] Then Saul said to Samuel, 'I have

sinned; I have indeed trans-
gressed the command of the
LORD and your words, because I
feared the people and listened to
their voice."

Saul feared the people more than he
feared God!

Now, Saul's request and action are even
more revealing. He asks Samuel to accompany
him home, so that he may worship the LORD.
Samuel responds that he will **not** return with
Saul, because he had rejected the word of the
LORD and He had rejected Saul as king.

As Samuel turned to leave, Saul tried to pre-
vent him from leaving by grabbing the edge of
his robe and it tore.

Samuel says to Saul, "The LORD has torn the
kingdom of Israel from you today and given it to
your neighbor, who is better than you."

In each statement and act, we learn more
about Saul. The text reads in

1 Samuel 15:30 (NASB), "30 Then
he said, 'I have sinned; *but* please
honor me now before the elders of
my people and before Israel, and

go back with me, that I may worship the Lord your God.'"

It's now clear that Saul is ultimately concerned with his own honor and pride, **not** God's honor or pride.

Samuel went back with Saul, but the damage was done!

Samuel then did what Saul would not do. He killed Agag, king of the Amalekites.

I will let this violence pass with little comment. I shall simply note that the Bible is a bloody book because God wants to highlight our violence, **not** His!

The final words of this chapter are tragic, but poignant.

> 1 Samuel 15:34-35 (NASB), "34 Then Samuel went to Ramah, but Saul went up to his house at Gibeah of Saul. 35 Samuel did not see Saul again until the day of his death; for Samuel grieved over Saul. And the Lord regretted that He had made Saul king over Israel."

All of this is leading up to Saul's betrayal of David.

CHAPTER 7

DAVID'S ANOINTING AS KING AND SERVICE IN SAUL'S COURT

1 Samuel 16:14-23

N ow we come to a turning point in this epic on the relationship between Saul, David, and YHWH. The text informs us that the Spirit of YHWH departed from Saul, and an evil spirit from YHWH troubled him.

Because we have a scientific, as opposed to a supernatural worldview, this makes little sense to us. If you want more information on this get Michael Heiser's book: *The Unseen World*. If you want to understand more about the work of God's Spirit in the Old Testament and the New Testament get my book *The Eight Ministries of the Holy Spirit.*

Because this book is not on the unseen world or the workings of the Spirit of God, I shall state as simply as possible what is taking place.

The kings of Israel were anointed with oil, which represented them being anointed with the Spirit. The Spirit anointed and empowered them to reign. In the Old Testament the anointing with the Spirit was more like being filled with the Spirit. The Holy Spirit did not permanently indwell people as He does New Testament believers. So, the departing of the Spirit means that His anointing and power to reign as king was gone.

The next words are even more confusing, because we have no teaching about the council of heaven, how evil spirits act, and how an evil spirit could be dispatched by God to trouble Saul. But, if you'll read 1 Kings 22:1-23, you will see that the prophet Micaiah pulls back the curtains of heaven and allows us to see what happens when certain decisions are made in heaven. God mediates the destruction of King Ahab, because of his evil. God is not arbitrarily deciding that Ahab should die, but the consequences of his choices are coming to bear, and God is involved in bringing that about. He asked for a volunteer from the spirits that are surrounding the throne. A spirit volunteers to go and be a lying spirit in the mouths of Ahab's prophets.

However, you interpret these difficult verses, one thing is clear: this is a turning point in the life and rule of Saul. That which is empowering his life is no longer the Spirit of God, but a spirit of evil. **Saul's jealousy and murderous intent towards David is not simply natural, but also supernatural.**

Jealous, hatred, and violence have evil, supernatural power.

CHAPTER 8

DAVID AND GOLIATH

1 Samuel 17:1-58

I n the last chapter, we saw the supernatural turning point in the life of Saul.

In this chapter, we will see the circumstances that lead to the natural or earthly turning point in the life of King Saul.

The story is very familiar to Bible readers. It is the story of David and Goliath. This story does not need to detain us, because we are not studying the exploits of David, but the jealousy and betrayal of King Saul against David.

Therefore, all we need to know is that King Saul and the Israelites were afraid of Goliath and the Philistine army. David, by the power of God and with an ancient slingshot, slew the giant and cut off his head with his own sword. There is so much teaching here. We could talk about how the two armies seem to be on two mountains representing the army of Satan and the army of God. We could talk about how God used the unlikely weapons of a shepherd boy to deliver Israel from their enemies. We could talk about how the giants of the Old Testament have a supernatural origin according to Genesis 6:1-4. We could talk about how the story points towards the Chief Shepherd, the Great Shepherd, and the Good Shepherd, Jesus, slaying the devil with the unlikely weapons of love and forgiveness. **But all we need to know is that David was the instrument of God's deliverance and his fame spread.**

CHAPTER 9

THE INCIDENT THAT MAKES DAVID SAUL'S OBSTACLE

The Beginning of Jealousy
1 Samuel 18:1-30

Now we come to the immediate circumstances that lead to the Saul's jealously and desire to kill David.

The soul of Jonathan was knit to the soul of David and Jonathan loved David as himself. Please keep in mind that Jonathan is the son of King Saul and heir to the throne.

From the day that David triumphed over Goliath, King Saul took David into his company or court.

We also get additional information on the relationship between Jonathan and David. Jonathan made a covenant with David and the elements of the covenant are powerful and instructive, but that's not our topic.

The text informs us that Saul put David over all the men of war, and this was pleasing in the sight of all the people and Saul's servants.

The next words of the text are the circumstantial turning point of this epic story.

> 1 Samuel 18:6-7 (NASB), "[6] It happened as they were coming, when David returned from killing the Philistine, that the women came out of all the cities of Israel, singing and dancing, to meet King Saul, with tambourines, with joy and with musical instruments. [7] The women sang as they played, and said, 'Saul has slain his thousands, And David his ten thousands.'"

This is all that happened! David didn't do anything negative against King Saul. In fact, we shall see that David was one of the most loyal subjects of Saul, but the singing of these women had a profound impact upon Saul. The impact is so profound and so important that I am going to include the text.

> 1 Samuel 18:8-9 (NASB), "[8] Then Saul became very angry, for this saying displeased him; and he said, 'They have ascribed to David ten thousands, but to me they have ascribed thousands. Now what more can he have but the kingdom?' [9] Saul looked at David with suspicion from that day on."

King Saul became suspicious of David! He is comparing himself to David and it seems that David is given more honor than he is given. His words suggest that David is out to steal the throne. He states, "Now what more can he have but the kingdom?" David's desire and attempt to usurp the throne is an illusion that was fabricated in the mind of Saul.

From that day forward, Saul watched David with suspicion and distrust—all because some women sang some words that he couldn't deal with.

Now we're ready to apply some of the words of my book, *The Blindness of Biblical*

Betrayal. We discussed how a model could become a rival and a rival could become a model. We discussed how mimetic rivalry, the imitated desire for the same things could precipitate rivalry. In this case, Saul wanted what he perceived that David had, i.e. the honor of being a valiant warrior, which was valuable to a king. Remember: he was unwilling to fight Goliath, but he wanted what David had acquired through Spirit-empowered warfare.

The text does not state this directly, but the whole story reeks of jealousy. I have explored and tried to determine the difference between jealousy and envy. I don't want to get sidetracked here, because it's very difficult to determine the difference between jealousy and envy, although some attempt to maintain a difference.

Saul's words and actions define "jealousy." *The WordWeb Pro 8.1 Dictionary* reads,

"Adjective: jealous

1. Strongly wanting someone else's position, advantages or possessions
2. Suspicious or unduly suspicious or fearful of being displaced by a rival
3. Protective and suspiciously watchful."

But David is <u>not</u> just Saul's rival, he becomes Saul's obstacle. Girard calls this metaphysical desire. "In Girard's view, **mimetic desire** (*i.e. the acquisitive human desire for what our models have*) may grow to such a degree, that a person may eventually desire to *be* his or her mentor.

This is seen in the field of publicity. Sometimes, consumers do **not** just desire a product for its inherent qualities, but rather, desire to *be* the celebrity that promotes such a product (*i.e. to be like Mike*). So, in **metaphysical desire** the disciple wants to be like the mentor and may come to want to be the mentor" (http://www.iep.utm.edu/girard/#SH2c).

While the closeness of a model and a disciple can lead to rivalry, "metaphysical desire leads a person **not** just to rivalry with her mentor, **but total obsession with and resentment of the mentor**. Consequently, the mentor becomes the main obstacle in the satisfaction of the person's metaphysical desire. Inasmuch as the person desires to *be* his mediator, such desire will never be satisfied. For nobody can be someone else" (http://www.iep.utm.edu/girard/#SH2c).

From this day forward, Saul's entire life purpose was to destroy David! He was blinded by anger, jealousy, illusions of persecution, etc., etc., etc. Remember the unreferenced quote of Girard, "We are never more blind, than when we are doing violence in the name of God!"

Saul needed to destroy David, because he had presumably set himself against the throne of Israel, in short, the throne of God. No one really knows why envy, jealousy, and rivalry develops in someone's heart, except the DNA of the Fall, and we don't have to do anything specific to precipitate those feelings. Saying one "No" to something a disciple wants or not giving ourselves to him/her can precipitate the **illusion** of being mistreated and may give rise to those feelings.

Again, in this case, the singing of some women precipitated jealousy, rivalry, and violence in the heart of Saul.

Consequently, I want to add my quote to Girard's quote. "We are never more blind than when we are doing violence in the name of God" and "We are never more blind or violent than when jealousy is driving us!"

Beware of natural passion and the demonically inspired passion of jealousy.

- Satan was jealous of God's sovereignty.
- Rachael was jealous of Leah's fertility.

- Joseph's brothers were jealousy of Jacob's favoritism.
- Aaron and Miriam were jealous of Moses' authority.
- The Chief Priests, Scribes, Sadducees, Pharisees, and even the disciples were, at times, jealous of Jesus.
- The Judeans were jealous of Paul's authority.

As I reviewed what the Bible had to say about jealousy, I discovered that the jealousy of God comes up repeatedly. Please understand that God's jealousy or passion over us is **not** human and is positive, as opposed to negative.

Also understand that even if God's jealousy was like ours, He is the only being in the universe who has the right to be jealous, because our existence flows from Him.

Alright, let's finish covering 1 Samuel 18.

The text informs us that the next day an evil spirit from God came mightily upon Saul. Notice the similarly of the language to the Spirit of God, i.e. specifically the words "came mightily upon."

David was playing the harp and Saul started to rage in anger. He happened to have a spear in his hand, which seemed to be often, so he hurled the spear at David with the intent of pinning him to the wall.

But David escaped from his presence twice. Now, there's something wrong here. Saul throws a spear at David once, but David goes back and allows it to happen again. Why would he do that? Answer: he's blind. My previous book is entitled: *The Blindness of Biblical Betrayal*. Not only is the perpetrator of violence blind, but so is the victim. On the cover of that book is two people shaking hands. One of those persons has a knife hidden behind his back. In addition, I had blindfolds placed on both persons, because the mechanism is so blinding that both perpetrator and victim are blinded.

I see this with most of the people that I try to help in this regard. When I suggest that the person trying to destroy them is jealous of them, most people can't process that possibility. They usually respond, "Why would they be jealous of me? I don't have anything that they should envy or be jealous of?" I imagine David responded the same way. He hadn't done anything against Saul. He didn't have any negative feelings in his heart against Saul.

But Saul's jealousy is based on an illusion and is demonically inspired!

The text goes on to inform us that Saul became afraid of David, because the Spirit of God had departed from him and had been given to David.

When our rivals see God blessing us and no longer blessing them, they may become afraid of us!

So, Saul removed David from his presence and demoted him, but David continued to be blessed because God was with him. This caused Saul to dread or become even more afraid of David, probably afraid that David was going to replace him on the throne of Israel.

Saul dreaded David, but Israel loved him. When the blessing of God is upon you, no enemy can turn circumstances against you.

Saul came up with an idea to get rid of David. He would offer his oldest daughter Merab to David, if he would go and fight the LORD's battles. He would send him into dangerous situations and hope that he would be killed in battle.

David was honored and said, "Who am I that I should be the king's son-in-law?" But when Merab should have been given to David, something happened, and she was given to another.

Now Saul's other daughter, Michal loved David. When Saul found out about Michal's love for David, he realized that he had another opportunity to get rid of David. He set the bride's price for Michal at 100 Philistine lives. David was honored and excited. Before the deadline, he had killed 300 Philistines.

But the plan to get rid of David backfired. David continually demonstrated his wisdom as a soldier in battle, and his fame continued to grow.

Even though enemies may be plotting our demise, when we are doing what God has called us to do—with a pure heart—no weapon formed against us can prosper and every mouth that is raised against us shall be ultimately silenced!

CHAPTER 10

SAUL PLANS TO KILL DAVID

1 Samuel 19:1-24

I n this chapter of the Bible, we see that David continues to be an obstacle and an obsession for Saul. Remember: Girard terms this obsession "metaphysical desire." "…metaphysical desire leads a person **not** just to rivalry with her mentor, **but total obsession with and resentment of the mentor**. Consequently, the mentor becomes the main obstacle in the satisfaction of the person's metaphysical desire. Inasmuch as the person desires to *be* his mediator, such desire will never be satisfied. For nobody can be someone else" (http://www.iep.utm.edu/girard/#SH2c).

The disciple renounces the model and wants to destroy the model. Both David, and particularly Saul, are blinded by the mechanism.

Now, Saul orders his son Jonathan and his servants to kill David, but Jonathan loved David and had created a close friendship with him.

Consequently, Jonathan warned David about Saul's plan to kill him, tells him to hide, and promises to find out Saul's latest instructions.

The next day, Jonathan talks to Saul about David and speaks well of him. Saul listens to Jonathan, vows that David shall not be put to death. So, Jonathan brings David to Saul and momentarily things return to normal. Yet, we know that the blindness of "metaphysical desire" is hiding something.

David again went to fight the Philistines and again God gave him victory. The text says, "Now there was an evil spirit from God on Saul and he again attempted to pin David to the wall with a spear, while David was playing the harp in the house." But David escaped and fled into the night. This is the third time that Saul has tried to kill David by throwing a spear at him. It illustrates the point that both Saul and David are blinded by the mechanism of mimetic desire and metaphysical desire.

There are going to be situations where people who are jealous of us promise that everything is alright and we will be blinded to the pattern of their behavior and trust them, but beware.

Then Saul sent messengers to David's house to watch for him so that they might kill him. It's interesting that the word "messengers" is a word that is commonly used for angels. These messengers were like evil angels of death.

Michal, who is David's wife and Saul's daughter, devises a scheme to help David escape.

Now David escaped to Samuel, who was at Ramah, and told him all that Saul was doing. And David and Samuel went and stayed at Naioth.

Word came to Saul that David was staying at Naioth, so Saul sent his messengers to Naioth to kill David, but when they saw Samuel standing and presiding over some prophets who were prophesying, the Spirit of God came upon them and they also prophesied.

This is not our subject, but in passing please note that the Holy Spirit came upon soldiers who were on a mission to kill David. I'm sure this is confusing, but the Holy Spirit's activity in the Old Testament is not well understood.

Three times Saul sent messengers to Naioth to kill David and three times the Spirit of God came on them and they prophesied.

Saul finally goes to Naioth himself and the Spirit of God came upon him along the way and he prophesied. When he reached Naioth, he stripped off his clothes and prophesied before Samuel. In fact, he lay naked all that day and night. Therefore, some were saying, "Is Saul among the prophets?"

Again, this is **not** the subject, but episodes like this impact people to believe that the prophets operated by ecstatic behavior, but that's not true. This is an isolated incident.

Nevertheless, God was protecting David through His own means.

God can protect us, even when powerful people seek to take our lives!

CHAPTER 11

THE COVENANT BETWEEN JONATHAN AND DAVID

1 Samuel 20:1-42

Now David fled from Naioth in Ramah and sought out Jonathan. He asked Jonathan, "What have I done or how have I sinned against Saul that he is seeking my life?" Jonathan said, "You are not going to die, because my father doesn't do anything without telling me and I know he wouldn't hide something like this from me."

David explains to Jonathan, "Your father knows that you love me and he doesn't want you to be grieved, so he has ordered that you not be told of his plans, but as the LORD lives and you live there is hardly a step between me and death!"

Jonathan says to David that whatever he wants from him he will do. David asks Jonathan to make an excuse for him not attending the new moon festival and see how Saul reacts, but if I'm worthy of death please kill me now.

Jonathan makes a covenant with David and vows to tell him what he finds out about Saul's plans. He wishes God's blessings upon David even as God had blessed his father, for Jonathan loved David as himself.

When David is not in his place the first day, Saul is patient, because he believes there must be a good reason. But when he is not in his place the second day, Saul's anger burned against Jonathan. The text reads in

> 1 Samuel 20:30-34 (NASB), "[30] Then Saul's anger burned against Jonathan and he said to him, 'You son of a perverse, rebellious woman! Do I not know that you are choosing the son of Jesse to your own shame and to the shame of your mother's nakedness? [31] For as long as the son of Jesse lives on the earth, neither you nor

your kingdom will be established. Therefore now, send and bring him to me, for he must surely die.' [32] But Jonathan answered Saul his father and said to him, 'Why should he be put to death? What has he done?' [33] Then Saul hurled his spear at him to strike him down; so Jonathan knew that his father had decided to put David to death. [34] Then Jonathan arose from the table in fierce anger, and did not eat food on the second day of the new moon, for he was grieved over David because his father had dishonored him."

Saul is so obsessed with killing David that he attempts to kill his own son and yet, he is blinded to how out of control his jealousy, rage, and murderous venom have become. I'm sure that Saul felt he was protecting God's throne. "We are never more blind than when we are doing violence in the name of God."

Jonathan went to inform David about Saul's intent to kill him and they say goodbye to each other with many tears. David departs and Jonathan goes back into the city.

CHAPTER 12

DAVID RUNS FROM SAUL

1 Samuel 21:1-15

In the next episode of this epic story, David went to Ahimelech the priest, who was living at Nob. Ahimelech came trembling to greet David and asked, "Why are you alone?" Ahimelech intuited that things were not normal.

David answered, "The king has sent me on a secret mission. Do you have anything to eat? We'll take five loaves of bread or anything else that you have."

The priest answered, "We don't have any ordinary bread, but we do have consecrated bread, if the young men have kept themselves from women."

David again answered, "I never allow the men to be with women when they are on a campaign.

And since they stay clean on ordinary trips, how much more on this one!"

The priests gave them bread that had been in the presence of the LORD, after it had been replaced by fresh bread.

Now, the text gives us a piece of important information: Doeg, the Edomite, who was the chief of Saul's shepherds happened to be there that same day.

David explained that since they left in such haste, they didn't bring any swords. Ahimelech remarked that all that they had was the sword of Goliath. David said, "There is none like it; give it to me."

Then David fled from Saul to Achish, King of Gath. But the servants of Achish were suspicious of David. They asked, "Is this not David the king of the land? Did they not sing, as they danced, 'Saul has slain his thousands, and David his tens of thousands?"

David heard what they said and since he was afraid of Achish, he feigned insanity before them.

Achish asked, "Why did you bring me this madman? Don't I have enough madmen in my presence? Shall I bring him into my house?"

Remember the short note that Doeg was there that day!

CHAPTER 13

PRIESTS SLAIN BECAUSE OF JEALOUSY

1 Samuel 22:1-23

David escapes to the cave of Adullam and when his brothers and all his father's household heard of it, they went down to him. In addition, everyone who was in distress, debt, or discontented gathered to David and he became their captain. They numbered about 400 men.

David left his father and mother with the King of Moab for their safety while he stayed in the stronghold.

The prophet Gad prophesied that David should leave the stronghold and go into the land of Judah. So, David departed and when to the forest of Hereth.

Then Saul heard that David had been discovered. He was sitting in Gibeah, under the tamarisk tree on the height with his spear in his hand and all his servants standing around him.

This is about the fourth time that Saul is depicted as having a spear in his hand. This does **not** seem normal to me. It seems he is obsessed with a weapon of war.

Think about it this way, "If you frequented a soldier or captain in the army who always seem to have a rifle or gun in his hand, what would that tell you?"

Saul begins to accuse his servants of conspiring against him. He states that his own son is conspiring with the enemy and no one will tell him what is going on.

At this point, Doeg offers up the information that he is aware of. He tells Saul he saw David interacting with Ahimelech. He states that Ahimelech inquired of the LORD for him, gave him provisions, and gave him the sword of Goliath the Philistine.

Doeg either lied, assumed that Ahimelech inquired of the LORD for David, or this information is left out of the text.

We can't tell yet, but Doeg's intention is probably evil. Saul's jealousy and obsession has impacted others around him.

Jealousy and betrayal are never con-fined to one or two persons, but they grow. Girard believed that "mimetic rivalry" grew until it threatened to destroy humanity in an all-against-all war. The Bible describes in Genesis 1-11 how violence covered the whole earth and God had to do something to keep it from destroying humanity. Here we see the conta-gious nature of rivalry, jealousy, and betrayal.

So, Saul had Ahimelech and all the priests of his household brought before him. Then Saul accused Ahimelech of conspiring against him and lying about it.

Ahimelech maintains his innocence and asks, "Who is more loyal than David and is this the first time that I have inquired of the LORD for him?" We don't know if Ahimelech inquired of the LORD for him or if he is saying, "Even if I did inquire of the LORD for him, it wouldn't be the first time."

Then Ahimelech protests, "Don't impute any conspiracy to us, because we don't know any-thing about this whole affair!"

But, the king said, "You and all your house-hold shall die!"

Saul orders his guards to kill Ahimelech and the priests, because they were conspiring with

David, but the guards refused to raise their hand against God's anointed priests.

Saul then turns to Doeg and orders him to kill Ahimelech and the priests. Doeg the Edomite turned around and killed Ahimelech and his relatives, a total of eighty-five men. Then he went to the city of the priests, i.e. city of Nob, and killed all the women, children, oxen, donkeys, and sheep.

Notice that the designation "Edomite" keeps coming up. The Edomites are descendants of Esau and their offspring were at war with the Israelites over time.

Jealousy can cause enemies to conspire against God's people! Would to God that we, i.e. God's people, would work together as quickly and easily as evil people work together against us.

But Abiathar, son of Ahimelech, escaped, fled to David and informed him of what had happened. David lamented, "I knew on the Day when we were with Ahimelech that Doeg would tell Saul. I am responsible for the death of your whole family. Stay with me. The one who seeks your life also seeks my life, but you will be safe with me."

CHAPTER 14

SAUL PURSUES DAVID

1 Samuel 23:1-29; 1 Samuel 25:44

The next incident is very interesting and instructive. David was informed that the Philistines were fighting against Keilah and plundering the threshing floors. Keilah was a city on the plains of Jordan. It was Israelite territory.

David inquired of the Lord, "Shall I go and attack the Philistines and deliver Keilah?" The Lord said to David, "Go and attack the Philistines and deliver Keilah?"

But, David's men said, "We are afraid here in Judah, we will be in even more danger if we go against the ranks of the Philistines."

So, David inquired of the Lord again and God said, "Arise, go down to Keilah, and I will give the Philistines into your hand." Hence, David went, fought against the Philistines, won a great victory, and delivered the people of Keilah!

Now the writer gives us additional information. Abiathar fled to David when he was fighting at Keilah. When he came, he had the ephod in his hand. This is not important to our study, but it's interesting that behind this ephod the sword of Goliath was hidden. So, it seems that the ephod was an implement of worship, as this was before David set up the ark of the covenant in Jerusalem.

When Saul heard that David had gone to Goliath, he opined, "God has delivered David into my hand, because he has entered into a city with double gates and bars." This is instructive. Saul believes that God has delivered David into his hand and that he is doing the will of God. Girard's quote comes up again, "We are never more blind than when we are doing violence in the name of God!"

Those who are jealous of us and seek to betray us will believe that they are doing the will of God. Those who crucified Jesus believed that they were doing God a favor. The blindness of betrayal is incredible! And the power that fuels betrayal, i.e. jealousy, is powerful!

"We are never more blind or violent than when jealousy is driving us!"

So, Saul summoned all the soldiers to go down to Keilah to besiege David and his men.

Now David knew that Saul was plotting against him, so he asks Abiathar to bring the ephod so that they could inquire of the LORD concerning what they should do. Consequently, he asks the LORD, "Will Saul come to Keilah?" The LORD answers, "He will come." David also ask, "Will the men of Keilah surrender me into the hands of Saul?" The LORD answers, "They will surrender you!"

Again, this is not our subject, but I'm impacted by David's ongoing consulting of God, even when everything seems to be against him.

We should never cease to pray and consult God, no matter who or what is against us.

So, David and his men, who now total about 600, arose and departed from Keilah. When Saul heard that they had left Keilah, he did **not** pursue David.

The next words of the text are wonderfully instructive.

> 1 Samuel 23:14 (NASB), "14 David stayed in the wilderness in the strongholds, and remained in the

hill country in the wilderness of Ziph. And Saul sought him every day, but God did not deliver him into his hand."

David's refuge was in the wilderness, in the strongholds, and in the hill country of the wilderness.

When we are being betrayed and attacked by our disciples, we will be in the wilderness. It is in the wilderness where we can be with God alone and where God will sustain us.

In the wilderness, we need to build strongholds or fortifications to protect ourselves from attack.

In the wilderness there is the hill country of prayer! Prayer and intimacy with God will protect us from the attack of the adversary.

Saul is obsessed with killing David. David has become an obstacle to the Saul's happiness and life. Saul sought David every day!

There are some enemies that will seek our destruction every day of their lives! I'm trying to alert you to that possibility, so that you will **not** be devastated if this should happen.

Please notice: God did not deliver David into the hands of Saul! David was walking in humility and following the direction of God and God protected him from Saul.

When we walk in humility and prayer, God will protect us from our enemies. I didn't say you wouldn't have to run. I didn't say you wouldn't have to hide. I didn't say that you wouldn't be sad and lonely in the wilderness. I said, "God will **not** allow our enemies to destroy us!"

Now David became aware that Saul was again hunting for him while he was in the wilderness of Ziph at Horesh.

Jonathan went to Horesh and encouraged him in God.

God will send some people to encourage you while you are under attack!

Jonathan also renewed his covenant with David.

There are some folks who are still in covenant with you. Don't allow the onslaught of the devil to blind you to the folks who are in covenant relationship with you!

Then the Ziphites went to Saul at Gibeah to inform him of David's whereabouts and to pledge their help in killing David.

The men of Ziph returned home ahead of Saul.

In the meantime, David and his men were in the wilderness of Maon. When Saul was informed of David's location, he pursued him there.

The next scene is interesting and ironic. Saul and his men were on one side of the mountain and David and his men were on the other side of the mountain. God wants us to see the stark difference between Saul and David. He wants us to see the difference between the jealousy of Saul and the honor of David. He wants us to see the obsession of Saul and David's reliance upon God. He wants us to see the mountain of difference between trying to grasp something that someone else has and relying on God to bless you with what He's got for you.

Saul and his men were surrounding David, when God interceded! A messenger came to inform Saul that the Philistines had made a raid on the land. So, Saul had to give up his pursuit of David and go meet the Philistines in battle.

When God is on your side, He will intercede when the enemy is closing in on you!

They called that place "The Rock of Escape" and David went up from there and stayed in the strongholds of Engedi.

Do you have a "Rock of Escape" in your story? Just keep living and you will, because betrayal is paradigmatic; it happens to everyone in leadership and in life.

CHAPTER 15

DAVID SPARES
SAUL'S LIFE

1 Samuel 24:1-22

I knew that most people would not want to read 23 chapters of the Bible and that would make a very long book. So, I have been narrating the epic story of Saul and David.

But there are some episodes that are worth quoting. This is one of them.

> 1 Samuel 24:1-7 (NASB), "¹ Now when Saul returned from pursuing the Philistines, he was told, saying, 'Behold, David is in the wilderness of Engedi.' ² Then Saul took three thousand chosen men from all Israel and went to

seek David and his men in front of the Rocks of the Wild Goats. [3] He came to the sheepfolds on the way, where there *was* a cave; and Saul went in to relieve himself. Now David and his men were sitting in the inner recesses of the cave. [4] The men of David said to him, 'Behold, *this is* the day of which the LORD said to you, "Behold; I am about to give your enemy into your hand, and you shall do to him as it seems good to you."' Then David arose and cut off the edge of Saul's robe secretly. [5] It came about afterward that David's conscience bothered him because he had cut off the edge of Saul's *robe.* [6] So he said to his men, 'Far be it from me because of the LORD that I should do this thing to my lord, the LORD's anointed, to stretch out my hand against him, since he is the LORD's anointed.' [7] David persuaded his men with *these* words and did not allow them to rise up against Saul.

And Saul arose, left the cave, and
went on *his* way."

You should be able to see by now that God
included all these chapters on Saul and David
in the sacred text, because He wants to teach
us about jealousy, betrayal, obsession, violence, etc.

Saul's whole life revolves around
killing David.

Yet, David can kill Saul and rid himself of
a vicious enemy. David's men believe this
opportunity is God's divine providence that
is in keeping with prophetic words. Have you
ever felt like God has delivered your enemy
into your hands?

But David did not read the situation in the
same way as his men. He rose and secretly
cut of the edge of Saul's robe and his conscience bothered him even about doing that.
Why? Because that which informed his conscience was different than that which informed
the conscience of his men.

In *The Blindness of Biblical Betrayal*, I
explain how mimetic rivalry can cause us to act
with the same violence that is being directed
towards us. We blindly imitate the violence of
our enemies, but David did **not** do this.

He explains his reasoning to his men. Even though Saul is chasing David all over the countryside, he refers to him as "my lord." David had a certain respect for and loyalty to Saul's office. He also calls him "the LORD's anointed." This makes no sense to us, because we think of anointing as the anointing of the Holy Spirit that has to do with salvation. David is talking about the anointing of the Spirit that makes Saul king. **Even though this doesn't make sense to us, Saul is occupying a sacred office and David will <u>not</u> raise his hand against him.**

There are times when our enemies will fall into our hands, but we must remember that they are God's creation and God may not be through with them in other contexts.

Not only did David not raise his hand against Saul, he prevented his men from raising their hands against Saul.

There will be times when we will need to keep others from acting violently on our behalf—even though they won't understand why!

After David left the cave, he called to Saul and asked him why he was listening to others who were saying, "David seeks to harm you"? He goes on to argue, "If I wanted to kill you, I had the opportunity. Here is the proof. I cut off the edge of your robe."

David's words are beautiful and instructive, but that is not what we are studying.

When David had finished speaking these words to Saul, Saul lifted up his voice and wept. He admits that David is more righteous than he is and that he has dealt wickedly with David. He asks the rhetorical question, "Who has the opportunity to kill his enemy and lets him go?" He implores God to reward David with good in return for what he had done for him.

Saul doesn't stop there but reveals an important realization. He says, "I know that you will be king, and the kingdom of Israel shall be established in your hand." I wonder when he came to this realization. At this moment or earlier? At any rate, he is seeking to kill David so that his own rule might be guaranteed.

Saul asked David to swear that he will not cut off his descendants and destroy his name from his father's household.

David swears, but he seems to have learned his lesson. Saul went home, but David went up to the stronghold. David now knows that Saul is obsessed with killing him and Saul's tears and nice speech will not change that.

Be careful! When someone has demonstrated that you are their obsession or obstacle, don't trust their peaceful overtures. "We are never more blind than when we are doing violence in the name of God" and "We are never more blind and violent than when we are driven by jealousy."

CHAPTER 16

DAVID AGAIN SPARES SAUL

1 Samuel 26:1-25

I find this hard to believe, but Saul again pursues David, when he is informed of his location in the wilderness of Ziph.

David sent spies to determine if Saul was coming and his location.

David and Abishai go to spy on Saul at night. When they come upon Saul's camp, Saul is sleep and General Abner and all the soldiers are around Saul.

Again, Abishai reasons that God has given Saul into their hands. In fact, in this instance, we shall see that God does seem to have given Saul into their hands, but Abishai and David are not on the same page with why God has given Saul into their hands. Notice how the text reads in

> 1 Samuel 26:8-12 (NASB), "[8] Then Abishai said to David, 'Today God has delivered your enemy into your hand; now therefore, please let me strike him with the spear to the ground with one stroke, and I will not strike him the second time.' [9] But David said to Abishai, 'Do not destroy him, for who can stretch out his hand against the LORD's anointed and be without guilt?' [10] David also said, 'As the LORD lives, surely the LORD will strike him, or his day will come that he dies, or he will go down into battle and perish. [11] The LORD forbid that I should stretch out my hand against the LORD's anointed; but now please take the spear that is at his head and the jug of water, and let us go.' [12] So David took the spear and the jug of water from *beside* Saul's head, and they went away, but no one saw or knew *it,* nor did any awake,

for they were all asleep, because
a sound sleep from the Lord had
fallen on them."

There are some great lessons in this text. David implies a truth in the question, "Who can stretch out his hand against the Lord's anointing and be without guilt?" Answer: no one!

Remember: what's right for you may be different than what's right for others.

In addition, David reasons, "His demise is in the hands of the Lord. It will come in its own time, but it will not come by my hand!" **David refused to return violence for violence.** That would have infected him and made him no better than Saul.

David is a great example for us to follow when we can avenge ourselves against our enemies. Put that vengeance in God's hands! Paul wrote in

Romans 12:19 (NASB), "19 Never
take your own revenge, beloved,
but leave room for the wrath *of
God,* for it is written, 'Vengeance is
Mine, I will repay,' says the Lord."

After David had put a good distance between him and the camp of Saul, he called out to the people and Abner. He charges them with being negligent in their duty to protect the king. He asks, "Where is the king's spear and water jug that were at his head?"

Saul recognizes David's voice and calls out, "Is that you David, my son?"

David responds affirmatively and gives the same impassioned plea that he gave the last time he had Saul's life in his hand.

Let's let the text give us the rest of this episode.

> 1 Samuel 26:21-25 (NASB), "[21] Then Saul said, 'I have sinned. Return, my son David, for I will not harm you again because my life was precious in your sight this day. Behold, I have played the fool and have committed a serious error.' [22] David replied, 'Behold the spear of the king! Now let one of the young men come over and take it. [23] The LORD will repay each man *for* his righteousness and his faithfulness; for the LORD delivered you into *my* hand today,

but I refused to stretch out my hand against the Lord's anointed. ²⁴ Now behold, as your life was highly valued in my sight this day, so may my life be highly valued in the sight of the LORD, and may He deliver me from all distress.' ²⁵ Then Saul said to David, 'Blessed are you, my son David; you will both accomplish much and surely prevail.' So David went on his way, and Saul returned to his place."

The lessons are the same, but God is repeating them for some reason—probably because of the blindness of the syndrome, which will keep us from being prepared.

CHAPTER 17

DAVID FLEES TO THE PHILISTINES

1 Samuel 27:1-4

We are coming to the end of this epic story and the ending in summarized in four short verses.

> 1 Samuel 27:1-4 (NASB), "[1] Then David said to himself, 'Now I will perish one day by the hand of Saul. There is nothing better for me than to escape into the land of the Philistines. Saul then will despair of searching for me anymore in all the territory of Israel, and I will escape from his hand.' [2] So David arose and crossed over,

he and the six hundred men who were with him, to Achish the son of Maoch, king of Gath. ³And David lived with Achish at Gath, he and his men, each with his household, *even* David with his two wives, Ahinoam the Jezreelitess, and Abigail the Carmelitess, Nabal's widow. ⁴Now it was told Saul that David had fled to Gath, so he no longer searched for him."

I did not attempt to calculate the period that is covered in this narrative, but I did go online and look for the answer. I found various answers: a year and four months; a year and eight months; four years; and eight years. Let it suffice to say that it was a long time and, yet, it's not until this point that David figures out the answer to his problems. He will leave Israelite territory and escape to the land of the Philistines. Why does it take him so long to figure this out?

I believe there were two reasons. One reason is the blindness of biblical betrayal. We have repeatedly discussed the blinding power of the mechanism. The second reason was the Israelites believed that their land was sacred, and David didn't want to leave the sacred land, because this would affect his ability to worship God.

We must pray for discernment when someone has become jealous, rivalrous, or obsessed with us.

CHAPTER 18

KING SAUL AND
THE MEDIUM

1 Samuel 28:1-25

There is a very interesting story in this chapter, but it only gives us a small bit of information about Saul and his betrayal. The text reads in

> 1 Samuel 28:5-7 (NASB), "⁵ When Saul saw the camp of the Philistines, he was afraid and his heart trembled greatly. ⁶ When Saul inquired of the Lord, the Lord did not answer him, either by dreams or by Urim or by prophets. ⁷ Then Saul said to his servants, 'Seek for me a woman who is

a medium, that I may go to her
and inquire of her.' And his servants said to him, 'Behold, there
is a woman who is a medium
at En-dor.'"

We see the deterioration of Saul's relationship with God. The Spirit of the Lord had
departed from him. The Spirit of the Lord
anointed him as king. Since that Spirit had
departed from him, for the host of reasons that
we have been listing, God would not answer
his inquiries.

So, Saul goes to inquire of a medium, who
appears to call up people from the dead! Again,
the writer is chronicling the deterioration of
Saul's character and loyalty to God.

CHAPTER 19

KING SAUL AND HIS SONS SLAIN

1 Samuel 31:1-13

I n this chapter, we come to the prophetic fulfillment of David's words. He said in

> 1 Samuel 26:8-10 (NASB), "¹⁰ David also said, 'As the LORD lives, surely the LORD will strike him, or his day will come that he dies, or he will go down into battle and perish."

That is exactly what happens. Saul dies in battle and the death is tragic in several ways. First, Saul commits suicide in battle. He falls on his own sword.

Second, the defeat is thorough. The text reads in

> 1 Samuel 31:6 (NASB), "[6] Thus Saul died with his three sons, his armor bearer, and all his men on that day together."

Third, when the men of Israel on the other side of the valley, and those who were beyond the Jordan, saw that the army had fled and Saul and his sons were dead, they abandoned the cities and fled. Then the Philistines came up and lived in them. Israel lost territory that had been won.

Fourth, when the Philistines came to strip the bodies, they found Saul and his three sons dead. They cut off Saul's head, stripped the body of its weapons, and sent those weapons throughout the land of the Philistines to carry the good news to the house of their idols and to the people. They put his weapons in the temple of Ashtaroth and fastened his body to the wall of Beth-shan.

David is avenged, but I'm sure he took no pleasure in the reality.

We may not see it, but God will take care of our enemies. May we be like David and not rejoice over the demise of our enemies.

Yet, even in their defeat, valiant men gave honor to Saul. The text reads in

> 1 Samuel 31:12-13 (NASB), "[12] all the valiant men rose and walked all night, and took the body of Saul and the bodies of his sons from the wall of Beth-shan, and they came to Jabesh and burned them there. [13] They took their bones and buried them under the tamarisk tree at Jabesh, and fasted seven days."

Are we valiant enough to honor those who have occupied certain leadership positions, even when they have been our enemies?

CHAPTER 20

SAUL'S POST-DEATH IMPACT UPON ISRAEL

2 Samuel 21:1-14

I n this chapter, we see that even after his death, Saul was still having a negative impact upon Israel. The first verse tells us all that we need to know concerning Saul's character and his ongoing impact upon Israel.

> 2 Samuel 21:1 (NASB), "¹ Now there was a famine in the days of David for three years, year after year; and David sought the presence of the LORD. And the LORD said, 'It is for Saul and his bloody house, because he put the Gibeonites to death.'"

Since this atrocity is **not** recorded until here, it makes you wonder what other atrocities might Saul have committed.

CHAPTER 21

THE CHRONICLER'S EVALUATION OF SAUL

1 Chronicles 10:1-14

In the Chronicles, we get a retelling of the last moments of Saul's life and an evaluation. Michael Heiser writes in *Brief Insights on Mastering the Bible*, "The chronicler rewrote the nation's history with an eye toward reminding his readers of what had led to the debacle: forsaking David and his heir, Solomon, and worshipping other gods. The forgiven nation must be loyal to David's dynasty. There was no room for rebellion. The nation must honor God's chosen line as it worshipped God alone. Toward motivating that loyalty, the chronicler's account presents David and Solomon at their best—the glory days of the nation—to make people want that good life once more."[2]

The evaluation is recorded in

> 1 Chronicles 10:13-14 (NASB), "[13] So Saul died for his trespass which he committed against the LORD, because of the word of the LORD which he did not keep; and also because he asked counsel of a medium, making inquiry *of it,* [14] and did not inquire of the LORD. Therefore He killed him and turned the kingdom to David the son of Jesse."

There were two occasions where Saul did not keep the word of the LORD: 1) when he intruded into the priesthood and offered burnt offerings; and 2) when he did not commit to **herem** or banning everything that was taken in a battle.

He consulted a medium when the LORD stopped answering his inquiries.

---

[2] Heiser, Michael S., *Brief Insights on Mastering the Bible (60-Second Scholar Series)* (p. 98). Zondervan Academic. Kindle Edition.

David had several personal failures, but He maintained believing loyalty to God. Saul didn't have many personal failures, but his actions revealed his disloyalty to God.

Therefore, God killed him and turned the kingdom to David the son of Jesse.

I will not take the time to debate or deconstruct the writer's view that God killed Saul. It is also apparent that Saul died from the consequences of his actions.

In an almost throw away comment by David, we learn something very important about Saul's time as king. When David was about to bring the ark of the Covenant from Kiriath-jearim to Jerusalem, the text records these words of David in

> 1 Chronicles 13:3 (NASB), "[3] and let us bring back the ark of our God to us, for we did not seek it in the days of Saul."

Traditional worship was missing during the days of Saul!

CHAPTER 22

DAVID LEARNS OF SAUL'S DEATH AND GRIEVES

2 Samuel 1:1-27

I mentioned earlier that David took no pleasure in the death of Saul. I gathered that from his overall actions towards Saul and from this chapter. This is an unusual chapter.

After Saul's defeat and death, a man came out of his camp to David. His clothes were torn, and he had dust on his head. He looked like he had been in battle.

He gave a different report about Saul's death. He changed one detail of the story. He said that Saul had fallen on his spear and was badly wounded. Saul asked who he was, and he answered, "I am an Amalekite." He reported that Saul asked him to kill him, because he was still alive. The Israelites were afraid of being tortured after capture.

The Amalekite testified, "Since I knew that he couldn't live, I killed him and took this stuff."

The Amalekite is probably shocked at David's response. David and his men tore their clothes, mourned, wept, and fasted until evening.

David asked the Amalekite, "Who are you and why were not afraid to touch the LORD'S anointed?" David ordered one of the young men to kill the Amalekite and said to him, "Your blood is on your own head, because you testified with your own mouth, 'I have killed the LORD'S anointed.'"

We know that the Amalekite was lying, perhaps looking to get some reward, because the death of Saul is recorded in 1 Samuel and in 1 Chronicles.

David wrote a beautiful song of lament for Saul and Jonathan. The text reads

> 2 Samuel 1:17-18 (NASB), "17 Then David chanted with this lament over Saul and Jonathan his son, 18 and he told *them* to teach the

sons of Judah *the song of* the bow; behold, it is written in the book of Jashar."

I pray that we will treat the death of our enemies with such grief!

CHAPTER 23

DAVID'S PRAYER CONCERNING KING SAUL

David prays concerning Saul and Doeg in Psalm 140:1-13.

I n Psalm 140, we have the prayer of David for protection from the wicked. It was evidently set to music for the choir director.

Verse 1 captures the heart of the prayer.

> Psalm 140:1 (NASB), "¹ Rescue me, O LORD, from evil men; Preserve me from violent men."

No evil or violent men are identified in the psalm, but the words surely include Saul.

I encourage you to consider these beautiful words and passionately rely upon God, when you are under attack.

We have come to the end of this epic story. God has included this mass of information because He wants us to see the syndrome of jealousy and betrayal.

We have seen that Saul becomes obsessed with killing David because of the singing of some women. David demonstrated great loyalty to Saul, but Saul was trapped in the illusion of offense.

He is blinded by his jealousy and his whole life revolves around chasing and killing David.

Even though David also shows some signs of blindness, he never succumbs to the violent feelings that drive Saul.

Saul's life ends in tragedy and David receives the throne as it has been prophesied.

I have written this book to illustrate the teaching of *The Blindness of Biblical Betrayal,* "We are never more blind than when we are doing violence in the name of God."

This has revealed another truth, "We are never more blind and violent than when we are driven by jealousy."

I have written this book to help you more accurately discern the biblical paradigm of betrayal.

I have written this book to help you prepare yourself by formulating realistic expectations about betrayal.

I have written this book that you might be valiant and victorious, through love and forgiveness, when your betrayal comes!

ABOUT THE AUTHOR

B ishop Flanvis Josephus (Joey) Johnson, II, is founder and senior pastor of The House of the Lord Church, founded March 6, 1974 in Akron, Ohio. The House of the Lord was founded with four members and has grown to a membership of over 7,000 and an average Sunday morning worship attendance of 740 in two services. The church, which started in a modest home, is an 89,614 square foot church plant, built around a 2,000-seat worship center. The church, along with the East Akron Neighborhood Development Corporation and Paul Testa, also co-owns a 47,000 square foot strip mall, across the street from the church, which houses retail space and 51 low-income, senior citizen apartments. All of this sits on 22 acres of land.

On March 5th, 2004, Bishop Johnson was consecrated to the bishopric by The Joint

College of African-American Pentecostal Bishops Congress and the honorary degree of Doctor of Divinity was conferred upon him.

Bishop Johnson has three honorary Doctorates.

He has been consistently rated as an excellent trainer and speaker by thousands of participants.

Bishop Johnson has been a part of many boards.

He was a contributor to the NIV Pastor's Bible, published by Group Publishing, in September 2000.

Bishop Johnson has written ten books.

Bishop was the founder, president, and instructor at Logos Bible Institute, which began in 1987. Logos offers a certificate for six semesters of New Testament Survey, Old Testament Survey, and Systematic Theology, plus a few electives.

He was also the founder and mentor of The Pastoral Mentoring Institute which began in January of 1993. The Pastoral Mentoring Institute existed to mentor leaders in Northeastern Ohio who were senior pastors, staff pastors, or those who had identified a pastoral call in their lives, through lecture, group discussion, practical exercises, coaching, counseling, support, and camaraderie to facilitate proficiency, confidence, and positive results in their pastorate, with a view towards the crown of glory.

Bishop was one of the founders of Emmanuel Christian Academy. This is a Christian School for grades Pre-kindergarten through eighth grade. Classes began on August 29, 1994.

In 2006, The Pastoral Mentoring Institute was updated to The Johnson Leadership Institute. In this Leadership Development Institute, Bishop hopes to prepare leaders to advance the reign of God, in all their spheres of influence, through covenant relationships that are driven by Kingdom-Principles or character principles.

Bishop Johnson has many other accomplishments and leadership appointments.

Bishop Johnson's mandate is to provoke deep biblical consideration of biblical realities that people habitually prefer not to consider. For more information go to:

www.bishopfjjohnsonministries.com

CPSIA information can be obtained
at www.ICGtesting.com
Printed in the USA
BVHW040253220120
570128BV00009B/170